synecdoche

Mark Young

Sandy Press

synevdoche by Mark Young

Cover illustration
With Magritte at Jindarie
by Mark Young

Cover preparation & design
by harry k stammer

ISBN: 979-8-9949368-2-5

Sandy Press
California
https://sandy-press.com/

sandypress@gmail.com

cont'd

cont'd

cont'd

Acknowledgements

A number of poems in this collection were first published in the following journals:

BlazeVOX, Blood + Honey, Bones: journal for the short verse, Cordite, dadakuku, Die Leere Mitte, First LiteraryReview – East, Fixator Press, Home Planet News, Ink Poetry, International Times, Lothlorien Poetry Journal, Misfitmagazine, Moss Trill, Petrichor, #Ranger, RIC Journal, Scud, Setu, Stink Eye Magazine, Stride, SurVision, Synchronized Chaos, The Prairie Review, The Saturday Paper, Unlikely Stories, Utriculi, Utsanga.it, & Version (9) Magazine.

My thanks to the respective editors.

Directions

I am using an astrolabe to
try to find out where I am.
There's no doubt it, by itself, is
unlikely to be of help, but it's
a great conversation starter.
People ask what it is, & I can
say to them: "It's a key to the
cosmos." Or: "Just a little some-

thing I found in a Marrakech
antique shop." We'll chat for a
while, then I add: "This is great
as a star map, but down here . . .
I'm looking to get to *XYZ*." & they
happily offer to take me there.

Later that night

The chocolate chip cookie's in-
vention was a happy accident.

We know this because of small
pieces of text sent to our browser

by a website we visited. They said:
"indelible ink is also inedible. Choc-

olate will help." Or maybe it was:
"kick dirt in his face & walk away."

Code can be difficult to decipher,
especially on an empty stomach.

The cost of flyovers

Même si les codes ne sont pas dépassés
they may display a profoundly
marked prostate, mainly above
1500 meters, with palm groves,
grain, & spices all mixed in. Are
you missing an important dia-
gnosis now that the anxiety level
of HK citizens has been pushed to

an historic high? The more you
tell us, the better -- even smart
guesses can help. You could
be rewarded with $99 tickets to
her New Zealand performance,
if your prostate's still up to it.

hung out

to dry, sometime be-

tween the solstice &

the lunar new year

hung out (2)

dry, somewhere be-

tween Yosemite &

the Four Horsemen

of the Apocalypse

Via Dolorosa

The wailing or
the wall, rising
clear out into
a corona of
crows' cries. Keys
synchronized with
paper shredders.
Transcribe the
debris. Un-
wanted amulets.

relentless pressure

Sometimes vermilion has a decon-
structed aesthetic. It wilts. Sad
flowers in a box. Is toxic to horses.

Signs of oral disease. Exposed foam
on the tongue. Just like Nike Blazers —
that new style, pretending to be old.

Jitneys were a form of hybrid be-
fore I was an Uber. Still are in
many places. An historical analogy.

Another one. A sunset cruise in a
convertible down a coastal highway.
Used to achieve rapid haemostasis.

A Chord — B Major

B onus

broccolini

badinage

blindspot

bandicoot

Bratislava

breakfast

xenophobia

D tale

dermatitis

dainty

disproportionate

dressage

demesne or demeanour

daguerrotype

Mandelbrot

F elated

feint

filibuster

flotsam &
I loved it
when he
went down
swinging.

flocculent

fulsome

flaccid

The Perils of Pauline

De jure legal, *de facto* legal, institutional, socially coded, the genres in vogue may present as a single organ disorder, blindingly exclusive & heteronormative. Common symptoms include retinal degeneration & polydactyly, but that extra digit doesn't make you see any better.

There's also orofacial dysmorphism where the tongue thins out, looks bald or shiny, becomes tender & sensitive to spicy foods. Not only means that singing those genres in vogue is contraindicated, but also that any rebates offered on solar installation are no longer available.

salad dweller

When it comes to debt ac-
cumulation, the young
lotus leaf, a new release
of the original 1913 edit-
ion, is ideal for industry
professionals & insurance
lawyers. It has served as
personal physician to Duke

Albert I of Saxony, & has a
single metal wheel mounted
on painted wood. Nearby, we
also have today a number
of helpful YouTube videos
crafted from my best recipes.

Episodic tarantulas

Then he said, "Behold now, I am old. I
do not know the day of my death." On

an average day 151,000 people die.
These famous people died in 2023 &

nobody noticed. What times we live in
that nobody missed her for more than

two years. Nobody I know is known
to have died. Life goes on unnoticed.

Trapezoid lunch pails

Never thought there'd be such
variety. All spacious enough to fit

two sleepers, a linguistic search
engine, & several large-sample

latent-variable structural equa-
tion models. Now all I need is

a sports car with a big enough
boot to keep a mid-life crisis in.

suffering solenoids

After rebuilding my bongo,
dry patches appeared on the

once-lush lawn. That's an
ongoing flaw in poppet de-

signs based on a mother's
behavior. We often suffer.

The hype, reactive

In hindsight, the subtypes
differ, a fault in the assay
perhaps, or creeping deter-
minism. Even if you win,
lottery tickets are a bad in-
vestment. You won't win all
the time; & in that time 50%
of your money goes down

the gurgler. Being struck by
lightning is more likely —
but before that happens,
as judgment of a unique e-
vent, consider a gift to help
make our mission possible.

A sedentary tailgate

My meniscus is torn. The
fluid in my iPad turns
tail & flees down long-
abandoned corridors. My
iPad turns purple & sets
off to find a *corrida de*
toros in order to sate its
blood lust. I am left alone
with only an ultrasound
machine for company. It
does not speak, is waiting
for a technician to arrive.

The / ibis are / out in force

The latest cyclone crosses the
coast near Bing Bong. The breaks

are negligible; &, before you know
it, Taylor Swift is back, her red lip-

stick perfect. Fences are being
erected to protect drivers.

TyouBE

Instead of writing one or
several poems — which is
what I should be doing —
I sidle into YouTube & into
a sequence of songs that —
effort for output — seems
much more productive,
even though it will end up

being a private poem. But,
hey, I'm in there singing
along, even if the only evi-
dence of that is some cryptic
reference in a public poem
written many months later.

In excess of the posted speed limit

Everyone going 80,
& I got bagged.

What does ; mean?
Either Spring is here :
or : calling out a function
using dot notation.

Decompose the outline
of complex parts. Vehe-
mence, pure undiluted
aggro, trollism, & per-
sonal axe-grinding.

What does that mean?
A bag of poo formed
by grinding down a pro-
fessional achievement.

It's official: Rizz is the
word of the year. A lot of
our language is gendered.

What Does Peace Mean?

A hierarchical hash verification

A person of deep conviction & principled
choices was unable to be reached yesterday
following an ugly confrontation at Brisbane
Airport's most exclusive lounge. Blame has
now been apportioned; but you can't just
point at everything that uses a Merkle tree &
call them blockheads or blockchain. Skilful
players use synonyms to avoid repeating
themselves, especially those accustomed
to the violincello. Please set your watches
for the return bout. We always back the fish.

Threatened / by a / plastic razor blade

Employers can eliminate the
frames of our back patio doors
& turn what could be a life-
threatening situation full of un-
necessary gimmicks into an
organ theme brimming with
allure. There are some draw-
backs — opening those doors
can produce epic sounding
pieces, but they do contain a
kind of darkness within them.

Nothing to merit treatment

What does Proverbs 26:24 mean? Metaphorically: *the glaze covering a clay pot may be attractive, but it's just a thin disguise*. She preferred *solar flares light up the undercarriage*. A battle of concepts. Fashion crime, thought crime — they don't break the law despite the will of the one who practices them. Some doc-

trines are intuitive, others invoke *Stare Decisis*, "let the decision stand," adhering to a precedent that determines the relative weight to be accorded to different cases. Always the chance of being more upset by the things that you didn't do.

from a past life

Rain, finally, after months of dry. Bucketing down. So dark I turn the lights on at 1.30 p.m. only to have them go out five minutes later as the power goes off. Thunder & lightning, directly overhead, only nanoseconds between flash & crash, not even enough time to say one thousand one. I sit in the open area beneath the house, some meters back but not far enough to escape the rain which sweeps in everywhere. I do not care. The gutters flood. Through a blurring curtain falling off the roof I watch the water start to lap over the edges of the pool. Ten minutes ago it was several centimeters lower down. The cat cowers under another chair. The turtles of the Woolwash Lagoon will be hurrying to lay their eggs. At the first sign of rain . . . Branches break off trees. There are no birds.

The storm moves away. The birds return. The power takes another twenty minutes.

Meanwhile, at the Kunstmuseum

A freight train goes by as I am
listening to Bach's *Air on the
G String*. It howls in the night.
Pizzicato cellos follow it through
at a walking pace. All vision im-
pairment stems from a simple
cause which has nothing to do
with the eyes. & then I'm in
Lithuania, in Vilnus, & an *a
cappella* choir tracks the same path
as the freight train. Home security
companies don't want you to find
out about this new device that is
cheaper, simpler, created by two
engineers from Australia, by which
time, in a baroque hall, a seated
string group line up behind some
very popular cellist & it's last year
in Marienbad, where a several hun-
dred voice male Mormon choir
tells me it's nearer my god to thee
which means we're heading back
to a basilica in Milan where Booker
T is dining out on a mix of green
onions & listening to some serious
players & I'm replaying all the
poems I've written over the years
that have Bach as counterpoint.

She was an oboe player in the Peloponnesian War

Salvage crews begin removing a block
of heavily armed infantry standing
shoulder to shoulder. I drive into town.
My cassette collection has disappeared.

I pass a grid planting of trees in a garden.
There is no command radius but is there
a spin limit? Column to phalanx, ultra
high density endcapping, thoracic skele-

ton with an acetabular articular facet; but
head-on against a similarly arrayed enemy
they couldn't exist without the shield. It's
hard to say who is most dangerous. Pike

animations still suggest a #MeToo reckon-
ing, but after articulating the manuscript
submitted by the dockside warehouse
it seems the tumor rarely presents in the

hand. That might be true; but she, usually
accompanied by her loyal trigger finger,
makes the most of her preferences by joy-
fully clicking the 'Cookie Settings' button.

The porterhouse diaspora

Spread out amongst an
eclectic mix of heritage &
modern buildings in the
heart of Sydney's CBD is
a 21st-century smoke joint,
considered to be the latest
& greatest missiology text.
Color, sound, taste, & di-
versity — but why can I see
only the ingredients? It may

be the year of the dragon; but
all that stands out is a post-
modern pastiche of punk
rock, glam rock, & a number
of cultural artifacts from its
own immediate past. It's a
poor manifestation of an ad-
diction to the Gothic & pop
culture. Calling it out is the
only thing we're doing right.

suppressed malarkey

The robocall message tells me to thank
the U.S. Supreme Court for reshaping
the sports betting landscape through
its decision that embryos are people,
have rights consistent with any person
living in the United States. That means
that embryos may soon be able to bet on
scripted WWE match results even if those
results were decided before conception,
& will still be deemed valid should an
abortion occur before the match ends &
there's a will naming the beneficiaries.

other than illicit acts

A common phrase among
scientists & students is that
a cartel exists, induced by
climatic & anthropogenic
factors, & that could quite
easily cause changes to the
serotoninergic & immune
systems of linguistic search
engines. But more research
is needed — another common
phrase from the same cohort.

the space provided

Electronic intrusion threat for preliminary
engineering studies to characterize the
marine mining of busty babes on big dicks.

Φ

Das ebenbürtige Herz moments with God
as First Aid to Mental Illness — the
thermodynamics of "Hold you, Mommy."

Φ

How to manage money. How to get the job
you really want. Persian literature in trans-
lation on problem housing estates in Britain.

Φ

The Theocritean element in the works of
a gay slave leaves a legacy of damnation.

Clustered at the end of a recent Google search were links which ended up pointing me to sites where the entry pages, despite the variety of legitimate-seeming domain names, were all similar with an 18+ warning on the front page &, when clicked upon, presented a message from the search provider that I would be risking life & limb if I entered. Still, poems can be shaped out of anything, including dodgy search results.

Surveillance astrolabes

In this rapidly evolving digital land-
scape, buying more than the necessary

amount of needed items simply says
you care less about saving money &/or

saving the planet than seizing each &
every opportunity to demonstrate how

important conspicuous consumption has
become in validating your way of life.

synecdoche

panzer
memories

entry points

mur-
mur-
ex

the Scilly Isles

"parachutes, my love,
could carry us higher"

Phoenicia

An / epic art / fraudster tells all

Here in the Tampa Bay area, the
big-eyed children — alluring,
at times unbelievable — deliver
a musical version of *caveat emptor*,
swinging easily into the melody
even though their grasp on the
words is a bit rough at times &
the wifi on the property isn't al-

ways effective. Still, being able
to sit in a lawn chair & listen to
intermittent music is better than
adhering to the mitigation hier-
archy. Maybe reset the network.
Or, perhaps, calm down, lie flat.

Olbers & the Okapi

The okapi survives
through excellent
camouflage. That
& the fact it is the

only antelope who
has ever puzzled
over Heinrich Ol-
bers's paradox —

if the universe is
infinite & full of
stars, why is the
sky dark at night?

After Max Ernst

The Elephant of the Celebes
stirs in its sleep & coughs

quietly. Bathyspheres im-
plode on the ocean floor.

Turbulence has your number

The unit uses censorship to quell dissent.

The unit is designed to create controversy
in a way that is likely to create public panic.

It has 762 direct competitors with more on the way.

Amongst them are self-professed experts whose
attempts at helping clients build clarity will only

deliver a reduced level of brain activity — anything

else is beyond their design abilities. The specter
of the censorship-industrial complex still looms.

11.03 a.m.

Wrote down what you said,
but didn't get around to
reading it. Maybe another
time. Today's not a good
day for it. Got to pack. Head-
ing south tomorrow, following
the whales down the coastline,
or at least as far as the coast-
line goes. To the promontory
that curls back on the bay
like an apostrophe. I'll see
what happens then. Could be
I stay there for the summer,
hibernating, or whatever
the seasonal equivalent
is. Reading. Walking. Watching
the divers go out for abalone.
Bring you back a souvenir
T-shirt. Or maybe I'll drift
to the city, see if I can find
that book on Art Nouveau
you've always wanted. Then
head north again, making sure
I read what I wrote down
earlier today. That way we can
pick up where we left off,
as if my migration was just
another pause for breath, one
more hole in a conversation.

In the plantain patch

The road that wraps around the
Conservatory is full of palanquins
parked end to end. Which is a
surprising fact given that there is

never anyone here in need of a ride;
&, even if there were, there are no
gharry drivers in sight on site to take
their place between the handles to

carry them away. The music that this
place is famous for has disappeared.
It reappears sometime later as comp-
anion to news footage that depicts a

procession of men carrying a convoy
of occupied palanquins behind some
marching band. Subsequent forensic
analysis reveals the footage is fake.

Curl, Sandbagged

A sedentary dog arrives sniffing
at the side door, possibly to see if
the wings the door bears have be-
come inelastic from that dip in the
bay this morning. Or, perhaps, some
icy hurricane blowing up from the
Southern Ocean might have left a
fanciful trail of avoirdupois in its
wake that will give some weight
to the parallel conceit that the fog
may equally come on big dog feet.

Convocation mountain

The school of forest medicine has
a thing for *strumpfhose* & those
initiation rituals of the medieval
guilds such as a slew of bobble heads
or zany ukulele ephemera. Its origins
are unclear. Some scholars theorize
long-term synergistic relationships;
others hold up ink-riddled feeds that
brim with the hashtag #QTTR & claim
itinerant tattooers are the points of ori-
gin. The regents call for calm, adhering
to their belief that all will be revealed
when the time capsule tucked behind a
plaque in the Cathedral is opened in 73
years. Until then, the only *diktat* is that
any & all balloons are to be prohibited.

Dawn in the Antipodes

The center of the cacaphony re-
bounds in my oesophagus. Birds &
antelopes await its outpourings,
eager for a first glimpse of the
morning menu. There is a storm

in the distance, disparate colors
blended together so that one is
unsure what the current color
is, what it was meant to be. A
poem by Tristan Tzara rides the

wall behind the bidet. It could be
about a winter in Patagonia; but,
equally, there are resonances of
the Tzar's assassination & the on-
going search for his missing child.

Semantic non sequiturs

Otherwise, there is no
otherwise, just an else-
where. No matter — both

are options, & each can

get you where you want
to go, even if you do end
up arriving upside down.

Lethe

Since I
no longer have
memorized
the ways
in which
words fit
together

it is with
some effort
that I
manage to
get these
few down.

& now they
are before
me I cannot
remember
what they
mean.

Meanwhile, in Fontainebleau

Baseball opening clashes with
fashion week this year. Diamonds
are no longer in. The uniforms are
a season out of date. Our sponsor
has their name emblazoned on my
bunt, what there is of it. *Goodyear*
reduced to *Goody*, & *ear* decorates
my crotch. My cleats stick in the
runway. I trip. My left areola shows
itself above the team name as if to
indicate how the vowel should
be pronounced. I do not add to the
scoreboard, let alone make it to first
base. One foot unnaturally placed a-
cross the other, I take my high-kneed
walk back to the dugout, to chew
gum, & have my hair brushed out.

The Handsome Pork-Butcher

For the past ten hours or so
the talking box of Francis Picabia
has been broadcasting Homer
in the classical Greek. I couldn't
follow it at first, only picked
up on it from the summations
of 'the story thus far' that
follow the station identification
which comes in after every six
stanzas. It looks like Troy won't
be able to hold out much longer.
I wonder what happens then.

Polyphonic snake beans

come high on the list of
UNESCO's indispensable

but essentially invisible
cultural heritage artifacts.

The Gates of Paradise

Dogs at the gates, alligators
in the conservatory — all part
of a playground for inhuman
resources. Within which, sing-
ing either in a descant or with
the assistance of a tight ankle
bracelet, impresarios line up
to offer services outside any

human rights laws. The key
shifts; now suitable only for
amoebae & a few axolotls. A
changed rhythm, also. We try
to sing along, a long song, in
an impossible counterpoint.

Grand Prix

My internet pro-
vider asks me
if I want to relive
all the highlights
of the 2024 V8
season. The
short answer is
no. The long answer
is that I never
lived them in
the first place. Nor
do I want to, live
or re-live, not even
at the end of
an evening where
I have gone round
& round the same
circuit without re-
sult. Boredom is not
for me whether it
be accompanied by
the smell of rubber
or the smell of
greasepaint or the
roar of the crowd.

A prologue for absinthe friends

If you feel it's time to fall in
love with a turn of the century
green fairy & sample the high

culture of St. Petersburg from a
Russian mosh pit, they are now
available in hardback. Both feat-

ure a medium weight & soft cotton
feel for your added comfort, use
cookies to improve the experience.

overflower

Pull the ball closer to you. Drop
your front hand. If there is lat-
eral movement, the clog could be
wedged further down the hole,
compromising an endpoint which
cyber criminals might then use
to explore an infected network.

L'oeuvre ethic

Cannelloni, cannula, cameleopard? Which one of?

Past the glass at breakneck speed. Unable to make out if it's the Vitruvian Man or the Vesuvian Woman.

Reflection in the glass, arms
    akimbo not en-
        compassed.

Therefore.

da Vinci with a pasta mustache. Duchamp the other *joueur d'échecs*.

R. Mutt in the doghouse, M. Lisa in the MTV awards. Pieces of.

For breakfast ate carrera cornflakes. Marble cake. Hey, cut out the voice-over. This is my video clip.

Stripped the bride bare. She was hot in the tail but oh so enigmatic.

Readymade.

If it's Tuesday we must be in Belgium.

Centrifungal farce

The yolks of two eggs, when
extended by tree resin with
antimicrobial properties, can
colonize about 90% of the pop-
ulation. To immunize against
it, my local medical center is
sharing two home remedies.

Both have great comic timing
& a scene-stealing cast. In one,
a plastic shaping tool lets you
alter a radish until it resembles
a post-apocalyptic 22nd century
curling iron. The other remedy,
given depth by a long marinade

of warm bottles of kombucha,
evokes Proustian memories. Soil
health is big business; but do cran-
berries cure urinary tract infections?

A done deal

He refused to talk
about the past. It's
a done deal he
would say, something
you cannot change
even if you wanted
to. That was the
public face. Privately

he was reinventing it,
rearranging it in a way
that made it more
palatable to remember,
more profitable for a
later presentation.

The lingering polyhedron

The word for the day is dodec-
ahedron. Why? Why not? It

sounds good, is reminiscent of
the age of the dinosaurs. A text-

book might easily now say "The
dodecahedron was twelve times

the size of T.Rex. Might have been
known as D.Rex, but preferred

the politics of the backroom, of
being the unseen power behind

the throne. Managed to miss the
meteor shower. Is still around."

Collateral dermatitis

Supposedly it's a straightforward
method of rapidly assessing
suspicious cellulose & fiber from
neutralized oats, using urea as the
active ingredient & strong mech-
anical agitation as a protocol that
has been codified as the standard,

but has anyone been able to extract
a glaive pattern from the evidence
board? Conservative management
is not a viable option. Some hacks
are like small village shops, can save
considerable time & effort. Not this
one. Localized side-effects make

finding patterns among the obscure
clues a harder task than putting a
jigsaw together when blindfolded.
The outermost protective layer col-
lapses. Xerotic dermatoses arise
that only colloidal oatmeal can al-
leviate. Life's like that sometimes.

Volcanized

ig-
norant

or else
unused to
the ways of
volcanoes

it is
riverrun
when lava
flows

run
do not stop
nor kneel
down

& say Lord
I am
thy faith-
ful servant

martyrdom
to ig-
neous
rock is so

ig-
noble

Capitulation will be tomorrow's song

Halfway through the movie, the
voice track shifts into Spanish,
the soundtrack becomes a caca-
phony of Panzer tanks while
images of them intermittently
appear that have little relevance
to the storyline. Then birds sur-
face on the windowsill, ballet
dancers replace the shots of
Panzers, & Shostakovich's *Jazz
Suite, Waltz No. 2* rolls out from
the wings to roll over & de-
molish the threatening tanks.

manganese petit mal

Despite the low penetration
resulting from bitumen aging,
& the fact that photo-oxidation

can speed up that aging process,
the *takaful* industry continues
to be nascent. Cyber cover is

making strong inroads into trad-
itional insurance; &, oh boy, don't
those beef tenderloins look amazing!

Möbius Trip

for Raymond Chandler & M.G. Escher

I have begun to write a novel.
Self-preservation. The room
is so cold I am in danger
of turning to ice. Already words
have frozen on my tongue,
thoughts have frozen
to my fingers. In the last
patch of brain still fluid
I see a novel as the most expedient
way of getting the blood running
again. It will be a crime novel
but not a police procedural or
psychological thriller. More
of a gangster melodrama. I am
a lazy writer; & the introduction
of a new character to maintain the flow
strikes me as being a far easier
task than striving to find some
perfect piece of descriptive
imagery. Just have someone
appear from behind a door
or out from the stand of trees on the
far side of the park. Toss a coin
for their being male or female,
young or old, holding or not holding
a gun — the choice is always
dichotomous. Now the room
is finally warming up. The novel
starts off: I have begun to
write a poem. The poem begins:
I have begun to write a novel.

Earth movers

I open the kitchen pantry
& let the ditchdigger out
for its evening run. It is
painted in pastels, as if to
say it is not just some fell
creature of the forest, has
culture, compassion, feels
for the earth each time it
tears it open to lay fiber

optic cables or waste or
water pipes. It claims it
has sensitivity, has read
poetry, is informed by
the poems of Edna St.
Vincent Millay & Emily
Dickinson. I half-believe
that — the poem bit, but
not the poets. Too often

I have opened the pan-
try door & found the
bucket raised, the crock-
ery & preserves smashed,
the digger turning semi-
circles, back & forth, back
& forth, & shouting at the
walls, "rage, rage, against
the dying of the light."

A / newt's first / law of motion

The problem
with being
amphibious
is I can never
remember
whether it's
the coach
driver or
the dive
coach that's
supposed
to be looking
after me.

On a Crimean Beachfront

The Oligarchs of the Black Sea
come whiffling down the esp-
lanade on their e-scooters. Spring
is here: which, incidentally, is the
title of a Rodgers & Hart song

about which & whom the OBSs
have no knowledge, especially of
the fact that, despite its title, it is a
sad song. Emotion has no place in
their portfolios unless sparked by the

acquisition by force of something
that belongs to someone else, & even
then they tend to be blasé. Usurp-
ation is a bit like Spring, something
that comes around on a regular basis.

Vox Populi, Vox Dei

I end up
watching
anime at
four in the
morning. *Cow-*
boy Bebop.

There is a
jazz sound-
track but in
my head
I hear Sinatra
singing "when

I was seven-
teen." It is
raining. It is
always raining
in anime. Out-
side & in.

inclemency

Hat turned up
against the
weather or was it
heat turned up
against the
winter or was it
heathens turning
up to support
the sinner or
was it the search
& rescue heli-
copter finally
turning up to
winch me out of
this inescapable
maelstrom I've
found myself in.

Deconstruction / Reconstruction

Robert Rauschenburg took
a Willem de Kooning nude
& rubbed it out to make the
point that all art is transitory.

Jorge Luis Borges tells of the
rewriting of *Don Quixote* in
a manner indistinguishable
from the original of Miguel

de Cervantes. Then there was
William Seward Burroughs
who cut up text, & rearranged
it in a different order in order

to create new texts. Who, when
describing the technique in a *Times*
Literary Supplement piece, attri-
buted it to a Lady Sutton-Smith.

Unencumbered by Cucumbers

Call me Ishmael. I am an
Unlikely donor to this
Collection of
User-chosen bric-à-brac that tends to
Render unto Caesar the things that are Caesar's
Before giving anything left over to
Institutions that cater for
The less fortunate members of
Society.

Avoiding the rumor mills

Nasturtiums bloom in the foot-
prints of an axolotl. It's a bit
like being caught up in a
Dylan Thomas poem — "light
breaks where no sun shines" —
but I'll feel somewhat silly pon-
tificating to a flower so much
further down the food chain.

They signed both documents

I like to eat either chicken or beef.
Neither is grammatically correct.
Which of those fur coats is yours?

This homemade chicken liver pâté
is a real hit. The mink style is often
associated with Hollywood. Mari-

lyn Monroe adored wearing real fur
coats, but wearing vintage fur can
be controversial. Consider getting a

coat in nutria (*Myocastor coypus Mo-
lina*), made from the fur of an intro-
duced noxious pest that is destroying

thousands of acres of southern US
wetlands. Have you asked about
the fur coat scam out of the trunk of

a BMW? Pâté is a French terrine of
seasoned ground meat. Some see it
as a way to honor the animal. Others

find it unethical & fill their capsule
cosy wardrobe with the new faux fur
line. Just $734, but often out of stock.

Concertina Bliss

Find the sunlight. Drink a glass
    of water. Drag the large
red pin with the dot to any desi-
    red location. As promised
by the realtor it's practically fail-
    proof & very easy to use.
That is, until the butterfly effect
    takes over or there's no
GPS signal, & a dense & busy sche-
    matic results. Metallic
gold foil may now glitter in the
    light; but how do you
communicate a circuit to a human?
    How does a defibrillator
work? How to demonstrate that
    each clustering algorithm
comes in two variants as stated in
    the client list that the att-
orney general says she has on her
    desk? Learning about sci-
ence can sometimes seem scary, so
    get that ebook for free now!

A good goodnight

The beggar
dines on the
color pages
of the Good
Food Guide.

Black lines &
white. On
the wall a
Franz Kline
painting.

Beautifully
painted. Badly
printed out. My
crappy laser.

The poem
from it
elsewhere.
Tension. Ex-
tension.

A weekend supplement
kept for a story
on the loss of
languages.

A piece of pseudo-
code from
Jukka.

The cat, the
night before her.

Open window.

The neighbor's
air-conditioner.

Open door.

Frogs, possums,
flying foxes.

Open encyclopedia.

Radium Hill to Ramsay.

Reading about rafflesia,
the stinking corpse lily,
the world's largest flower.

Thinking about
ragas & ragtime,
the rhythmic
in-betweens.

Next to the Kline
a Chinese print
of some Japanese
calligraphy.

Washed-through
color. $6.99 at
the Remainder Shop.

Mass-produced.
But. Majesty.

Oh to have a
chop hand-
carved
from hard-
wood to
sign my
name with.

Red ink, or blue?

The night
behind me.

One lump, or two?

Wandering

Proved true for
a / particular
value. If. Then.
Likewise holds for
others in the
sequence. Is
mathematical in-
duction. Is primary.
Not just for numbers
but anything that's
linked. Stones &
bones. Things in the
earth, or growing in
or going on it. One
truth discovered,
the rest will follow.
Sometimes in
the pith of
sugar cane you
might find ivory,
a wizard's mojo.

Cantaloupe reciprocity

The whipped cream isn't especially sweet
but its structural relationship with the
ancestral *cucurbitaceae* karyotype is so intense
I sometimes have to remember to breathe. Give

it a sniff. If that blossom end doesn't smell
like meritorious firecrackers, it's better to go
into a cave & cool off. Everyone who isn't
brown also gets terrorized now… is it still not

your fight? Tactfully accessorize with airy
jewelry, wide-brimmed hats, & UV filtering
sunglasses otherwise you will be considered
to have the energy of a squirrel that's discove-

red a coffee plantation. You like my boat? A
sweet silhouette in black reads as cool summer
goth. It will be revealed down the line if Mar-
got Robbie will return to play Harley Quinn.

Slightly belligerent

The presence of new actors in modern asymmetric conflicts calls for visual aids that can significantly enhance understanding. It's important to foster an environment in which the skills & dispositions associated with those

axiomatic rules of war can be updated to allow complex information to be visually navigated so that dynamic spaces exist for interactive problem solving.

licorice trigonometry

The law of cosines states that
the square of any side of a stick
of licorice can be recast as an au-
bergine whose rhyming structure
follows that of a pantoum or, oc-
casionally presents its entirety as
if it were a ballade conceived by
François Villon. "But where are

the snows of yesteryear?" you
might ask, only to realize a lick of
licorice later that they can be black
as often as they are white, depen-
ding on the relationship between
their sides.

bonsai propaganda

I've been working on myself since
I turned thirteen, a librarian lost
in the wasteland, contemplating
the conflation of religion with racist
nationalism. All the lines, shapes,
& illustrations stemming from this
are drawn as vector graphics. I have
six wind chimes in total now; it is

essential to match your brand ide-
ntity. So, color palette, tone of voice,
font face — line them up like ducks
in a row. Not for yourself but for
others to applaud. What they pick,
combined, may partner your persona.

Fame & fable

It seems that many of the
inventors still talked about
never saw their work brought
into being — take da Vinci's
lens grinder, Babbage's Diffe-
rence Engine. Others talked,
made things, but never existed.
Are equally celebrated for the

failures of their fables. Such as
Daedalus who has a plinth to
himself — the wings with wax
which melted & cast Icarus
into the sea, the labyrinth on
Crete unraveled by a thread.

Directly South of the City

It's such a weird place —
think hand-crafted mosaic
crosses done in sophisti-
cated shades of pink, white,
& brown. It's slightly dis-
gusting — think Tab Hunter
playing at being macho. It's
a long-term proposition &
many simply lose interest
after a few years — think
17-year-old clarinet players.

The Game of Gulf

In the Royal &
Abstract Science of
space & quantity
it transpired
we were equally
matched. That's a
therefore or a
turning point. Let's
go dancing, she
said, & so we did.

Paranoid Poem # 4,375,169

My new you
beaut anti-
virus program –
2007 version –

(& which, since
installation, brings
on go slows or
even freezing) scans

my infernal machine
& tells me
it has detected
a tracking cookie.

"Low threat status"
says the report.
"Recommend
ignore." But

ignorance is
not bliss to the
committed
paranoid, so I

fix it & sally
forth into the
ether sans
worms, sans virii,

sans cookie.
I do not
trawl the web,
rather step

delicately, as if
in a field of
glass. A brief
visit here &

there, check
my mail, de-
lete the spam —
though if it

wasn't for the fact
that it's been
done so many
times before

I could get
some good
poems from the
subject lines —

& then with-
draw, but not
without running
another scan.

The tracking
cookie is
back in the
jar again! So

I revisit
the journey, a
slow waltz, step
scan scan, &

decide it's my
email account
that's probably
the culprit

which makes
sense since
I recently read
that various

government
agencies in
concert with
various inter-

net providers
are in the
process of
building up

databases of
everybody's
virtual travel
& cyber-

correspondence.
But what can I
do about it?
Somehow I don't

think that broad-
band wrapped
in alfoil would
have that much

effect &, besides,
it's the forces
of law & ordure
that are lined

up against me.
So I decide
to join them
whilst at the

same time pay
homage to the
comics & b&w
serials that

nourished my
youth. Have
changed my
email address.

From now on
I can be reached
at Mark Young
at G-man_dot_com.

12.20.2006

What to do (when the nematodes swarm)

You have to start somewhere. We all
knit with a different technique. Cooler
paint colors help the walls to recede.

This breathing room is crucial. It serves
as a practical resting spot for extra fluid,
explains what the five love languages are

in a language that isn't one of them, a
general phenomenon that has nothing to
do with the Baader-Meinhof phenomenon.

Lack of sleep can make staying in bed
tempting, trying to gauge how long before
the concierge starts to admit the crowd

gathered in the lobby waiting for words
of wisdom from you or your autograph.

Au clair de la lune

Came out
in a Pierrot
costume

powdered face
frilled collaret
white blouse
with large
buttons

expecting
to be
introducing
a *Commedia*
dell'Arte
performance

Right time
wrong place —

propelled
center-
stage into the
Spanish
Inquisition

Spoke
only the
one phrase

et
in
Arcadia
ego

Sufficient
heresy

Burned
as a
witch

by
characters
dressed

even more
gayly
than I

lemon centered

To aid in constructing a short
historical overview of community
membership & its desire for a
legacy — no matter how far-
reaching the impact — proper
hazard recognition, even when
released in mystery blind boxes,
is fundamental. Entropy always

increases when anti-leptons are
annihilated; &, in this epoch of
recombination, the possibility
of a closed universe, oscillating
forever, means that gravity may
eventually block any expansion.

transcendental medication

Because electrons are shared evenly
their symmetry has a kind of beauty,
producing 'patterns' that one thinks
can be identified. This inclination to
find patterns often carries over, even
when dealing with unrelated inform-
ation, is even applied to polarization
curves that do not form dipoles. There

are several strategies that can be used
to change such pattern thinking which
often comes from overheating through
having too many active apps. A simple
& effective one is to set the current to
zero. The system soon stops bubbling.

Nostalgia Treadmill

Unless you were a prisoner
& the machine was designed
by Sir William Cubitt, life on
a treadmill was fairly simple
before TikTok came along. "The
12-3-30 workout is a low-imp-
act cardio workout. Set the
treadmill to a 12% incline &
walk 3 miles per hour for 30
minutes." No longer enough.
Now you have to dance on
them, preferably in tandem
with a friend on a parallel
machine, or wear the latest
fashion, or light a few candles
& walk on the treadmill at a
gentle pace in your pyjamas
with a cup of tea. 'Cosio cardio'
it's called. You can even repli-
cate making your way through
an airport with a backpack on,
speeding up if you're scared you
might miss your flight. A song
rises unbidden from my murky
mental depths. "The 12-3-30's
been & gone, doo-da, doo-da,"
sung to the melody of Stephen
Foster's 1850 *Camptown Races*.
Puts it in its temporal place. That
might be an anachronistic atti-
tude, & now politically incorrect,
but, hey, I'm sure you get the drift.

riffles on the river

#1
I crossed the creek at the
back of my property. Two
weeks passed before he

realized it was not he who
had avoided her. The day had
cooled, & the meadows were

bright with flowers & spring
grass. Against the late sun his
skin looked bathed in iodine.

#2
The copper wire had been un-
wrapped from the head of a

broom. A motorcycle turned
into my drive. People were

swimming laps in the pool,
stroking through the electric

columns of light. The wind
was still warm & I could smell

the water that had just been re-
leased from the irrigation ditch.

#3
It rained hard, blowing in sheets
across the fields & against the
side of the house. It was quiet
for a long time, then I heard his

engine start up. An image regis-
tered in the corner of my eye, one
that connected somehow with
memory & dreams. The sidewalk

was marbled with the green &
pink neon of the marquee. I put on
my pinstriped beige suit. He wore
a blue suit & tie & white shirt.

#4
He reached behind him &
closed the front door. The sun

was almost down & the square
seemed filled with a soft blue

glow. I could see the iron tethe-
ring rings that bled rust out of

the old elevated sidewalks. The
courtroom was almost empty.

#5
Under an empty dome of yellow
sky, the wind popped in his ears

as though it was filled with distant
pistol reports. Inside the small

stucco church, on the walls by the
Stations of the Cross, electric fans

oscillated. They all seemed to fun-
ction with an orderly purpose from

which he was excluded. Fifteen
minutes later, a power failure dark-

ened the building for three hours.

[Source text *Cimarron Rose* by James Lee Burke]

64 Js + 2 for Jukka-Pekka Kervinen

jongleur jurassic jingle jaguar jalousie jade jabiru jigger
jerry juxtapose juice jemadar jaffa juryrig jolt jonquil
jersey juggernaut jam joke jettison jockey joie jihad
jazz jest jinx jetsam jerkin juvenile jess joint jolly
jain jacaranda jag jonah jibe jetty japan jacobite
jereboam jemmy jung jewel jingo jilt janitor
jerusalem jester juggle jostle journal julep
javelin justice jeopardy jargon jersey
joust justify jerboa jodhpurs junk
hajj

Those Character Arcs

The seemingly innocent romantic gesture of a young man
has been hailed as a model for Public-Private partnerships —
some people simply never go anywhere empty-handed.

He was watching *The Princess Diaries,* an innovative,
provocative conversation on all aspects of religion. The
fact is great films have been made with great characters

that do not change who they are at their core. It would be
even better if he were British. They can invest in beautiful
umbrellas because they know they'll never just be left

in a cupboard unused. & does anyone know where you
can get those umbrellas where the outer part is gray,
but the inside (rain-free side if you like) has the sky on it?

Time / still moves / while standing still

Is political time, is archipelago
time. "Why should we have
half the islands on one time &
the other half on another when
they're only fifteen minutes apart?"
So some adjusted the local IDL
with an eastern bulge while others
moved it westwards. On Taveuni

Island, in the Fiji archipelago, one
can stand across the actual Prime
Meridian, have one foot in today, the
other in yesterday. Then, without
moving an inch, have one foot in to-
morrow while still balancing in today.

Fender Bender

A within-subjects study is investi-
gating whether using multidose
vials or old-school flash cards is

more efficacious. Both are some-
what pointless, & may be hazardous.
Even dead batteries can still produce

some electricity. It's why, to overcome
its innate low speeds, a Pokémon of
Sassy nature welcomes Bitter berries.

Off or on the nomads' track

Salamanders gamboled outside as he
dined on radicchio & the deep-fried
antennae of microwave satellites. Else-
where there was birdsong, & titles
embroidered on the red caps of elderly
travelers escaping their Winnebago in
search of lunch. He recognized none
of the proffered titles — not that that
mattered. Some languages were never
meant to become the common tongue.

Majority Foreign Owned Meat Packers

We will always protect our American
bananas, even though we cannot
build them, said the artistic director

of the Sante Fe all-boy ballet company.
It is our God-given right, & the left
will never take it away from us. They

pirouetted prior to glissading offstage,
slipped on a banana skin, & are now
being treated for fractured vertebrae.

positronic bagels

I love how it turned out, a
mesmerizing world of glitch
that is now considered one
of the top ten best piercing
salons in Ozaukee County.

The Vladivostok Funicular Railway

would be considered as just another
Trans-Siberian Orchestra cover band
were it not for its custom-made Y-sub

connector with a Y-shaped metal shell
& parallel contact rows that sometimes
presents as a remarkably lifelike imit-

ation of a nineteenth-century French up-
right piano & sometimes as the grand-
daddy of all multilingual ouija boards.

Lackluster ski_p_ants

Baits are the way to go, especially
when they have reinforced knees

& hems, & snow gaiters for proper
function. A question asked of Trump's

Truth Social AI partner confirmed
this solution, but added the rider

that neither ants nor ski pants had
introduced the President to Jacob

Epstein & that the model for *The
Rock Drill* was well past puberty.

Bona Fides

When I entered the country, I told the immigration authorities I was a gatherer of bones, a polisher of stones, adding that I didn't mind if the activities were reversed. They were sceptical at first, doubting that these were legitimate occupations, but a search confirmed it so they let me in, muttering that there were cemeteries for the first, rivers for the second, that if I didn't find a job within three months I would be deported.

When I applied at the employment office their records revealed that it had been years since they'd last had a vacancy for the line of work I laid claim to. In the meantime however, there were part time jobs available in either an ossuary or a quarry that might help keep my hand in while I waited.

Which is how I wound up cataloguing storage bins of bones. A set of threes — three floors of a building in the old part of town, a common repository for the relics of three orthodox religions, & which encompassed at least three centuries of active accumulation. It was an eclectic collection, incorporating anything that had the slightest connection with the religions without concern as to the provenance of the items. In the first few days I recorded five femurs supposed to have come from the one saint, discovered that polydactylism seemed to be a prerequisite for beatitude, that to become a patriarch in the fifteenth & sixteenth centuries demanded a bone in the penis. I was especially intrigued by the relics of someone identified only by a sigil, whom I nicknamed Saint Fibonacci because of the way the number of his metacarpals seemed to increase, & who, it was rumored, wasn't even dead yet.

Despite all this I started out with good intentions, sought diligently for the correctly labeled specimens to complete skeletons which were then interred in perspex coffins in a reliquary that had been specifically built for this purpose several years before. Then expediency — & the fact that there were so many unidentified bones lying around — took over. I began to fill in missing parts, but still maintained the integrity of my own records, staying clear of scientific fraud in my determination to become the Bertillon of bones. But the fact that the papers I wrote appeared in non-paying journals whilst the reliquary drew an ever-increasing number of customers finally changed my attitude.

I began selling to traditional Chinese medicine outlets bone fragments guaranteed to extend life expectancy. I crossed over from *The Journal of the Proceedings of The International Conference of Osteopaths* to *The Southern Enquiring Truth* with articles such as "Widespread syndactylism a generation removed disproves the myths surrounding Saint Epimenides the Celibate." & then the activity which caused my dismissal, bringing out a calendar in which each page featured the bones of a saint whose day fell within the month, probably because of the context in which I placed them: "Miss July seeks solace with the ulna of St. Theophrastus."

I have been working at the quarry for three months now. Very soon, a burial plot for a previously unknown schismatic seventeenth century sect will be discovered, complete with contemporary artifacts, their age able to be confirmed by carbon dating. I have learnt well.

Random / noises from / the vowel house

According to onlookers, I'd
dodged a bullet. But I've been
deep into word puzzles of
late, & couldn't let that pass
by without questioning how it
parsed. "Do you mean I may
have dodged a ballet since I
didn't go into the city with my
partner last night? Or maybe
didn't spend that same time
watching a belly dancer or that
comedian who provokes belly
laughs in his audience? Or,
more precisely, perhaps no
one offered me a glass of Bellet
wine or took me for a drive in
their old Isuzu Bellet? Then
again, nobody offered me an
overnight billet, or gazed at me
& sent me billets-doux, or in-
vited me to go & see that
French pop group that's app-
arently quite popular these
days. Have I left anything
out?" I get blank looks, so re-
mind them that bollets are
another word for a type of
mushroom, & that it's now
dinner time, & I've prattled on
for so long they're probably
wishing that the projectile had
hit the mark & stopped me
carrying on like a bull at a gate.

An old note from Wikipedia finishes off an unfinished old poem

If I used the jargon of the
business pages, I would begin
by saying that telcos fall out
of the sky with the regularity
of space debris. My economics
textbooks tell me this happens
because telephony is a market
with perfect competition, where
players enter when it seems there
are opportunities, & fail because
there soon become too many &
the smaller ones cannot survive.

Those failures can be spectacular.
The entry capital is often weak.
Each time a player collapses
one of the smaller players sets out
to seize at least a part of its
customer base. Froggy is one
such player, & makes great use
of sky writing. Weekends I
often see the ephemeral slogan
froggy.com.au blow away.

Today I am deep in thought
struggling to write a poem about
images. I go out to smoke
a cigarette — I should use a macro
to record that line I use it
often enough — & see Froggy in the sky.
My mind wanders. I substitute
Froggy for lines from songs & poems.

Froggy one so true . . .
Froggy, I'm with you in Rockland . . .
Froggy in the sky with diamonds . . .
What's it all about, Froggy?

Where have you gone, Joe DiFroggyo?

The founder of internet service provider Froggy was sentenced in the District Court in Sydney yesterday to 21 months in custody with 12 months non-parole for lying to finance brokers.

Australian Financial Review, Apr 16, 2004.

DNR

Tomorrow I will turn
off the life support

on the cauliflower. The
florets are starting to

darken, gangrene is
setting in, what point

is there in amputation
if it's just going to re-

main a vegetable for
the rest of its life.

Rotory ho'

Caught by a sudden
sideways gust of wind
as it comes in to land
on the White House
lawn, the President's
helicopter veers off
course & decapitates
all the reporters wait-
ing to capture today's

five seconds of risible
inanity. The President
beams when he finally
alights & sees the head-
less chickens. He hadn't
wanted to answer their
questions anyway, too
many other things on
his mind. Like the re-

cent G-up summit, &
the radical no-shelves
no-books plan for his
retirement Presidential
Library. &, of course,
world domination, his
master plan sharpied
out as just one line on
one page — 1 + ? = 2.

Tranquility in high heels

The atrium is / full of
lust but otherwise is
overflowing. Trains
leave on the hour as
the third hand of the
conductor comes
sweeping down to try
& guess the sequential
value of the prizes. Order.
Or a musical sweet. Try

treat. Or suite. Or segue
into sequins with a
secondhand train that
sweeps across the piazza
& takes the money with
three items still left
open. Cannot see the
fingers on the keys,
but the thumbs are
those of a murderer.

frayed reins

The lengths of crossing loops are
a limiting factor that is becoming
more frequent & severe now that
all orders are processed in Denmark.
Network vulnerabilities arise. One
only has to read this year's cyber
security report to see how easily
they can be exploited by a malicious

actor to compromise security. Else-
where the Sixers are building to-
wards their best as the finals race
heats up; but it seems that the 76ers'
fatal flaw, a brittle health, will again
threaten their championship chances.

escalator elephants

Australia Post has issued an urgent warning to residents to remain on high alert as the risk of "porch pirates" starts to rise.

Scientists have found a fix for the increasing amount of space junk.

*

Archaeologists discover the world's oldest paintings, made long before human existence — & strikingly advanced.

Trump hires a new architect for his ~~$300M~~ $400M White House ballroom.

*

Joe Rogan recently told the American Alchemy podcast that AI-powered machines could one day have a 'virgin birth,' creating advanced robots, or 'offspring,' capable of performing real-world miracles using technology.

Australian Labor Government's new AI plan puts faith in self-regulation.

*

'Good decision.' Trump hails controversial health plan as an advisory panel appointed by Trump's vaccine-skeptic health secretary Robert F. Kennedy Jr. voted to end a decades-old health recommendation affecting newborns.

Vanity Fair and Olivia Nuzzi announced Friday that they have agreed to go their separate ways following a flood of new revelations about her romantic relationship with Robert F. Kennedy Jr., including allegations of journalistic ethics breaches.

*

Trump family is inflicting a new kind of Saudi-style 'royalism' on the US.

Arrests as apple crumble, custard thrown at UK crown jewels.

*

Anger as National Parks grant free access on Trump's birthday — & end it for MLK day.

NATO state to declare state of emergency next week, Lithuanian PM says.

x3

Nostalgia sets in, & I lose my
teeth. More benefit than hind-
erance — stops me chewing
over *un temps perdu* that has
little to make it worth revisiting.

Nostalgia sets in, & I lose my
internet connection. Maybe I
shouldn't be piggybacking into
the ether on my neighbor's wifi.

Nostalgia sets in, & I lose my
canteloupes. Not immediately;
but before the melon harvest
can get underway, gargoyles
that have torn themselves away
from cathedral roofs flock down
to feast, leave nothing behind.

Seasonal

Broad brushstrokes
of smoke across
the landscape. Point-
illist pain in my
head, just behind
the ear. Everything
closes in, is
focused. Nothing
I can do but
cut myself another
slice of watermelon,
lie back, &
think of England.

Can't hold

Candlelight &
Candlemas — the
words swing
lightly in their

hammocks. Not
so Candelabra. That
gutteral ending
sleeps on the floor.

from a book of the hours

4 a.m.

black blink black black blink
blink blink black blink black
blink blink blink black blink rem
blink black black blink blink
blink blink blink black black
black blink black blink black ember

5 a.m.

— but not
Magritte clouds
but proto-
poems hanging
in the not-
blue sky, but
not in reach —

6 a.m.

piss proud
piss long
piss hard
piss it all
away
— absolution

trapeze equivalents

My Fender is fully hollow, but has
painted on faux F holes. It also
has the basic physical vocabulary of

aerial arts embedded in it, a standard
created in Europe for the exchange
of routes, stops, timetables, & fares. So

many different ropes to choose from!
Party food catering, engineered for
both safety & performance, is avail-

able for an additional cost predicated
from an economic analysis based on a
large number of patient-level surveys.

discombobulated bluegrass sessions

Roots music is rising. No flashy
bells & whistles darting in & out.

Instead, tricky finger-picking pat-
terns prioritized, & regular claw-

hammer banjo workshops in a
hall just across from the local pool.

Does anyone still remember school
lunches in Minnesota in the 1970s?

For Miss M

cat kookaburra
late-night owl

the
avariciousness
of another
avatar

attacked by
angry ants &
in defense
a self-
inflicted
mortal blow

attempting
to emulate
the Worm
Ouroboros

auto-erotic
asphyxiation

Pantechnicon nightmares

From the next room I hear
"a dead body in the whore-
house" mentioned on the
YouTube channel that who-
ever is in there is watching.
I think I've misheard, laugh
it off. My ears have become
somewhat flaky since driving
behind a large furniture van —
articulated in two places rat-
her than one — for several
hours & finally finding my-
self stranded in nowhere Ari-
zona. A rather strange place
to end up, considering I had
started the trip on a winding
road that led up into those
mountains in the center of the
South Island of New Zealand.

Glacial

Nothing moves. An
ice shelf crashes
into the sea. Nothing

moves. A single wave.
Pause. Resurface. A
second wave. The up-

ward thrust is smaller
now. Third wave. Nothing
moves. Float. Jetté.

Pirouette on a point
determined by the
center of mass. Nothing.

Moves.

www.ingramcontent.com/pod-product-compliance
Lightning Source LLC
LaVergne TN
LVHW090532110826
845146LV00003B/1065

9798994936825